To Lynda

As Always

Contents

I.

Those In Peril

Apache Rain

My scout vanishes.
All I see is the rain
thatching his nape,
the half-kick his god dog always gives
at a gulley's welcome.
Then he's lost in that red throat,
one of the land's hundred thousand.

Something is awake beyond this ridge,
something we didn't care to see
yesterday, when we fanned out,
skittered our dots of life across these uplands –
when we bore down where hot ground
and cooled air meet
in staggers of mist.

I hear my scout's clatter.
Any moment now
his head will present below me,
his back will arc over those night-blue flanks.
But he stops.
Something has him in its thread.

Yesterday I didn't dare gaze out,
unmanned as I was by fear,
my heart blown aside
by a wind that uproots one history
and throws down the hookings of another.

Something is awake beyond this ridge,
and now I try
but the thicks of rain
are across my head,
gumming my eyes,

their casual curtains tight
on every blink.

I must look with my ears–
at voices now, sudden, children's, our children's,
rushing us,
bowling past me like delinquent scrub.
How did they get from camp?
How did they slip the obedience hand
while the other hand fell to its stitching?

I blink again.
Their cries mob my scout,
sting his god dog's confusion
up on its hind-legs.
Something is awake beyond this ridge
and it is theirs, and they know.
Their voices kick, tumble, fade,
back-heeling all our old moons and powers.
My scout cries.
I hear the dark
fighting to outfall the rain.
A light from no gentle heaven
comes hot on my face,
with machined music,
with other voices, thrumming
in colours no moon ever warned of.
I get my eyes open and see...
all that bred me to this instant crisped away...
and see.

god dog: the Apache term for a horse.

Shannon

dark channel
thick weather
weak signal
no headland
cars grating
dogs whining
bar bursting
sky melting
hunched lookout
doused starboard
clouds laughing
kids asking
kids whining
kids crying
dogs rolling
cars melting
air bursting
black channel
no lookout
no signal

Uninsured

Heaven's eye takes pictures
the street was never graded to bear:
a lagoon enchantment,
figures lolling astern,
trailing a fear apiece like hands
in an August bay.
Lily-pads wheel over suck-holes,
play doorsteppers,
play crown-the-lintel.

Upstairs, a terrace of life
is dry a touch longer.
Keepsakes hold their story
inches apart,
knowing their shapes
by the shapes they are not,
respecting how each other
fell off the back of affection
into evermores of dust.
Upstairs is still summer,
a proffered kiss,
a bad calculation
evened with courteous regret.

Downstairs is unmaking.
Bolts are away like minnows
from a wafering hulk;
glue sighs thanks
that its clench of dowel and mortise
is revoked.
Plates, coasters are deepwater eyes
bleared with electrics,
the oak-smoke of irregular flex,
the pilot-light's tango,
the nine, eight, seven before all hell.

Chicken Little the Kitchen Guy
(All makes and ranges supplied and installed)

There are many versions of the 'Chicken Little' fable, but the basic premise is that a chicken eats lunch one day, and believes the sky is falling down because an acorn falls on its head while it's dining.

I'm in the wrong line of work.
It breaks my heart
to sass gravity,
lock ceiling tiles unshiftably in place,
fettle the shaft of a carousel
so nothing spooks the rotation.
People don't know what they want.
Their kitchens should be
a tireless bounce
of trim and durable;
their walk-in closets
should walk out and buckle
as puppets unstring for death;
their lazy susans
should be that precisely,
saucering through domestic air
like the spin of an archangel's tyre.

They should want gravid skies,
the ballyhoo of constellations
fire-whipping their princessy swirls,
their bo-peep finishes.

Yesterday I braced an island counter
at the reach of its pride.
It's probably just as I left it,
stilling the bubble of spirit at the mark,
no whiff of tilt or prophecy of kindling.

The picture makes me cry.
My tears, at least, plunge earthwards.

Man from Johannesburg, Woman from Portadown

I am a white from Johannesburg.

History throws its boots

into the corner of my voice,

spills apart the vents of its tunic,

presenting its arse

to a fire of hair and fingernails;

my speech

is the alternate thuck and ping

of its gobfroth in a spittoon,

its buttons discharged

from a belly of equatorial girth.

I married a woman from Portadown.

Her voice is bullets:

her solace for this one's bones in their twilight,

her enquiry after that one's kid,

flash holes across brocade and anaglypta

like the scamper of blooded feet

in overnight snow.

So we keep to ourselves,

live moments

others have just vacated,

twine in shadow
till some stranger's hurry
echoes from the street.

We mean no harm,
would gladly dip our wing
at the soft disturbances
of chance joke or blether;
but are enfeoffed
to the monsters undying on our tongues--
re-breathing dawn assaults
in our murmurs,
taking the mere seconds of a yawn
to winch cargoes of stopped mortality
up the arm of a streetlamp,
leaving any time of sun or moon as chooses
to prink the kirtles of tar,
the gouts of feather.

Safer to make love with rags in our mouths.
Safest to cry in silence.

The Secrets of Stage-Fighting

I tickle and worm fatality
from the dust-silvered air.
My sword cuts the backcloth
at your ears, pricks light
into the figurements
of Bear and Orion.
Your shoulders weave back
on the count of misery,
hoping to close on a false panel,
to follow your shins and torso south
down a trap. Poor bones.
Their distant feet stay stood
one shuffle adrift from mine
(which I spread a touch,
distributing the bulk of my intent
for when my arm shoots back,
tips into its own conclusive business).

Any second now
I shall break in upon your last good meal,
consumed, no doubt, in careless vacancy;
make you the eastern and western fringe
of my blade's intimate horizon.

Then all will be fool's-gold showers:

cuckolder into maggot pie,

traitor into bulged hessian

as if strung on a barn-joist,

weeping docks and chaffage

at the end of a pennypinched harvest.

Prepare. Your ghosts clamour

at the hundred doors of your body.

They must fly, as from ground

runnelled up in filth. . .

... now the hilted gaps in my hand

should sing the click, the safe rattle,

as my steel retreats from its jest of dispatch.

The glow of my eyes should die into a wink,

unbinding yours from terror.

But I am lost at the bottom of this moment.

You have been too seductive – as quisling, footpad,

enemy of the sun. I cannot unbelieve you.

Pickings and Spoilings

A lone man on the sands,
clothes given up for all-comer winds
to balloon and whirl
as on a dummy with a disappeared face
in a January window.

He watches the tides
bail in their pickings and spoilings:
dead screens
with the last bubble of high days
in their deeps; bills ungrubbied
by any fleet hand
from the years when the world
cracked wise in exchange and surety.

Here's something:
a knight of old, dying,
earpiece pendant
from a mouth that suckered rumour
till it was true as magic
and he strolled away
from casino evenings
jingling the numbers to somebody else's life.

His armour falls ahead of him

into the rock-pools: fussy little extras, palm-wide,

that bleed ampersands and runes,

toowit their last,

dial out of a game beyond playing.

The man with the whirled clothes

shifts off his mark

and picks one up. He could be

a Burgundy farmer

turning up a flint-head

in a time of guillotine edicts

he doesn't know about either.

The gizmo frets.

The letters of one saved message

go out like lights

after sweeping-time,

when brooms fall like duellists

in cupboarded black.

The Girl from Midfoxfields

The girl from Midfoxfields kneels
with hair tumbled
against the parish bounds

day has folded itself
into one late window:
a fire-breach
clefting night's breath upon the town

nothing else only sightless things
that swivel and commote
in the black hour

one finds the girl's arm
battens and feeds
swags pendulously off
as if it's mulched its own sting--
not knowing it has taken
of a body built from tears.

That morning, she fancied
a carriage ploughed her washbowl—

spokes played gilded hoop-and-stick
from one mirrored eye to the other.
Prophecy bound her brows together
a seed split in her deeps.

She saw herself
in a time of ruffs and acreage
other hands took on the winter of her veins
stayed her foot
till her floor was scoured
debouched her tea
into gauzy china.

She leaned at the pantry window.
Was that the pastor at the yard-end
swart as Midfoxfield's dancing-man?
Did he know?
Did he have a shining lad
downwind of his piety
ready to walk through the very walls
at her, a hill of pork pies in his arms
a baton of manor deeds in his pocket?

Continued overleaf

As she stared
she peeled an apple for the haying-pot
till the blade got loose
among her untended rhythms –
she saw the lad's face
in the stipple of welts –
the pantry became
an affair of blood and kisses.
But no-one came
to speak stars among her shadows
Midfoxfields sat on
like an egg in a tray of ashes
its people the usual stalks
moving as though they could not
as though the streets instead
skulked past them.
Beyond the garden-field
the haymakers' guts
passed a grumble around
like rusty bitters
her mother's call fell unjumped-at
among the pantry-board pips and skins
the washbowl at last
upped and sank the girl's face
to its enamelled bed.

So she hunkers now
where Midfoxfields hangs up its name
the vision dries on her collar
and flakes from her breasts
the years to come are at her as before
with boot and flail.

Why should she raise a knee?
Why should she turn an eye
or her blooded hand ever again
to the shuttered
chestnut-dripping county?

Never A Bone Between Them

Do they know their boy
is up at his window,
high where the air
misremembers the feathering of larks
and first stars
find each other shyly
with their horns of antique light?

Do they hear the town strike nine?
See the September day
fall itself apart,
hand over its narrows of blue,
the crackle of a leaf new-dead
in a flowing tree?

Their boy frets and squeezes
against the pane. Makes a passing feint
at the catch, as if giving
a lollopy wave
to his purseful of words and summers.

Do they know that,
held for now on the sill's twigging,
the thin cuppage of glass,
adventure makes his eyes
wetly beautiful?

Tails of spent comets glide
from one eye to the other, the vapour-fleece
of unbuildable jets.
All the come-hither of space works upon him.
Words with never a bone between them
twangle his heart. Boing. Kerpow. Splat.

Below, a bus strikes a can.
It ballerinas sleepily to rest where it meant.
A wrapper fights lamp and rail
yet homes like kite-silk to its pavestone.

Do they know his hand and the catch
are of a length?

He is blessed, being rubber,
being boots that crunch flame and calamity
and keep their sheen.
He clamps a harness of speedlines
to his back. The wind writes whoosh
up the frames and bricking,
knuckles his mouth,
cries it again in his soul.

A day bed in Bern

"The patient always makes the last act - swallowing the drug or opening
a valve of a drip himself."
('Dignitas', BBC News Online, 20 01 03)

　1

This is the umpteenth time

me on the bottom step,
thickly there in the well
of beaded mats, phone clutter,
my fingers at the lounge-handle,
pattering unfallen rain into my head

upstairs, my shadow stands
jilted, broken into a wagging ear,
a single furrow, smoke-eyes, green and grey –
sucking all the chimestrikes of air
into its cry
that I am still hunting for something;
watching me where I stall
at the evening level of a street
whose name, these days, fiddles its sounds,

dumps them anyhow
into the ringing bowl of memory

2

I run out on me.
In shops, at work,
traced by bodies who say dad
or use me with adjacent familiarity,
I see myself
with a shoulder hard to my eyes' quarterlights,
a boot up, scraping the devilish sill –
bending the bars
as a hunter throws off tropic lushness.
I catch the slide and foot-thump,
the liberty run. Strain to the last of me,
packed sand on a heel disappearing

3

I fall over,
shred the webbing
of the man who loved to carry me,
to rock on neat-splayed heels,
skim caps onto hall pegs.
Find that the world
has vandalized its law
and I am shinnying rugs,
going stiff or limp
in the meltwaters of physics,

Continued overleaf

gazing at dust-balls,
picks of cat-biscuit
that must have known my feet
when they tamped out their ground
one swing ahead of me,
dusting up echoes
that became the anchored sun
and whatever shape of day
blushed out of it

4

Last night – some night –
my wife came in,
draped every inch of the house
with a stranger's presumption.
I stood as if bagged
in a dust-sheet.
A score of faces
circled her head, eyes everywhere,
howling after bolted spirits –
then fell as a shake of embers
and let her be. A tear stole home
to her underlip

5

In the time remaining,
I watch the oval whirl
of my perpetual spaces –
slack and coat-flapped

at the back of the early bus,
cane-tight on the train.
At night, when bus and train
have the going stripped out of them,
my spaces loop on
like creatureless blood,
their paternoster sureness
inviting me, any time,
to step in and out of my razor-cut
or collar-ringed self.

They flow past the window,
their breezes thumbing the curtain-braid.
My pillows go over and under.
I ravel, hard as the sobbing
locked up in my wife's back

      6
I have never been there.
I imagine a poster-paint canton,
a city of hotel doors
ajar on fitments of efficient weave,
rules of awkward insistence.
My palms sweat,

Continued overleaf

ready to gum passport to ticket,
ticket to document,
document to letter:
a crest in modest relief,
a valediction made fast in three languages.

I stare through that flourish –
see a kindly man of my years,
hair long defeated,

spectacles trapping and dealing
the twinkles of noon.
An assistant, too –
younger, her urge to severity
laid just beyond the brush of her fingers
for my hour's sake.

I have no idea how.
A dewdrop swagging its mercy
on a pin's end. A tablet
stroked through my lips
as a magician might phhht
a boiled egg, a florin
lobbed from row T.

Where will I be then,
on the daybed,
in the soft snows
of those few moments after?

Years back from all this –
from the first double-bump
in my engine room,
the first time a gear
faddled on a jut of steel
and refused its hole.
I shall be... ten.
She will be the nit-nurse.
He will be the district panel-man,
the god next door,
discreating with his yesterday,
his tomorrow smile.
'Right as a trivet,' he'll whisper,
as the two of them align and step away

7

Trivet.
I shall roll sideways,
knees to chest,
my hands closed on nothing,
the corner of that word
in my mouth

Terraplane

I could mention I saw a bat
that it cut and poured evening onto its wing
jumped the quarries of air
ran its lanes like a country mortician
called late to the back of beyond
clattering on his black waistcoat

that it made colour lose its nerve
pinned fence to branch to stone
dragged the night from inside them

lay easy a moment
on nothing
imprinting masteries of jack and dive
for hunter-birds to recover
all over again at first light

a terraplane, I could call it
shucking carriageway dirt
from its underplates
rising
to where the placemen of creation
sit on clouds
weigh their measured heaps
of anger, wind, calamity
then flip their palms
loosing each at its naked mark

terraplane,
I almost say
almost turning
to the lightless walls of the house

but she strides unhearing
tightens a line of inventory
with each twist of the keys on her finger

soon she'll be gone
strewing pictures of us
from an uncommitting hand
soon after
the rooms will be tanks of echo
squared hard round finality

tomorrow night
there'll be the windows only
no-one to see them seeing
that bear the wide fidget of ivy
catch maybe a single loop of a bat
and forget

waiting for rain and leaf-ghosts
to fuss at the back of other lives.

What did Mr Morgan do?

What did Mr Morgan do
on Monday nights
in term time ...

... after we'd unconfined him
and, oh god, he could
hop off in his Ford Popular
sheltered again
from having to be
the spirit of Junior 4
and throw his teacherness
to the four mildewed corners
of the room
where even the lice
in the dying desks
had to forage in time
to eight eights
and the Punjab's roll-call
of who lived there
who fanned themselves
on the slabs of ex-palaces
what they turned out
how it was freighted
from one bit of used-to-be-pink
to another
and Prester John
who had only one side
to his woodcut face

fired himself at the margin
like a lupine sprinter
brandished a stave or a gun
or some such to give destiny
a poke?

Did Mr Morgan sit on Monday nights
at a table in a lounge
with paperwork
and the ebbing smell
of a rissole treat under his nose?
Did he look up
at an open bookshelf
jutted into the room
ploughing space
like a weirdly-strung galleon
tricked out in bowls
flatulent with Parma violets
lamp fitments
squeezed into Drambuie necks
a Guernsey remembrance
that sloshed its beak in water
straightened its copper-wound spine
and fell to again?

Continued overleaf

Did his wife have a beehive
did Love Me Tender
peck at her head
as she smoothed a plan
to lock nephews up in wool?

Who appeared on their tank of a screen?
Ghostwoman, incanting
always, always wash your hands?
Robin Hood stooped commanderish
in the cup of a black-white forest?

Did Mr Morgan
stretch his back
feel like a bullet
stopped between gun and termination
wondering how he'd got to this chair
and was there, please, a place for him
no messing
beyond our belts and gingham

our germ-happy coins for inedible meat,
the life-cycles, Saxon villages,
stars prodigal on paintings and backs of legs
oh god, our everyway dumbness?

II.

Batmans Hill, South Staffordshire, 1961–1972

But the dead themselves cannot forgive.
They cannot relieve us of our fury
that they should have disappeared,
leaving us to clear up the mess.

Terry Eagleton, *The Gatekeeper: A Memoir*
(London: Penguin, 2001), p.8.

Always and everywhere,
this unequal struggle to preserve and remember.

Ian Jack, *The Country Formerly Known As Great Britain*
(London: Vintage, 2009), p.325.

Dew That Missed Its Morning
(1972)

I

the place you grew up in
told nothing

roads with their bad meld of borough tar
never ran towards the world's heart

no Delphic shake
from the cricket club wall

though you stared by the hour
a Pied Piper tagalong, sleep-fooled, shoeless

it talked only in babypads of moss
readied its long inward topple

but still you go back
get in among the kerbs and porches

lean over the end fence
where that jacaranda

was braced by poles and banisters
more and stouter as summers flew

whose house was it? whose idea
to traffic such beauty

jag it down in this unloveliness
lock up its delta spirit to eat itself unseen?

just two poles now
squiring a play-frame

II

up and down you go
round all that old outstation
human feathers caught on hooks
nests of the unflown

still you listen with your skin
for words in those flaking adjacencies

words that knew
how you should have become

which journey-star
should have rounded your eye
when you struck out

they might still be there
swagged on a carriage-lamp's underspike
like dew that missed its morning

III

surely they were there
back in the square heat
of old-money summers
blew across the screaming life
of gangs, jubblies, nettles, diverted mud—
ready to fill you
when you caught breath
cast about for the shapes
to fasten across the next hour
ready to fall against a careless window
come at you in sleep

IV

but no words now
aerials and lamp-necks
stop divvying up their horizons
and stare you away

no sound
save the usual scraps
from the engine-hours:
footsteps gaining
on a throb in their owners' heads
somewhere the combustion
of one perch and two magpies

say your words found a readier home
laying back on another kid's river

say you'd have done as well
to climb the sad jacaranda
under a Buzz Aldrin moon
suck down all the sky-going static
get wise any-old-how.

Not that it would have mattered.
If you shake your ears clean,
break in on any grove of life,
you'll find no-one knows anything

save that time pulls and elbows through
pretending to be a doctor

best go
or it'll have to be the train after next
coming for you in the dark

Outside

(1961)

Why don't you go outside?
Rain has bagged up its pearl whispers.
Sun jags hard at the patio,
whose slabs my father has left
to find their own horizons.

Stuck in here all day.
Music and cooled shadow,
ways of being loved before I knew it.

You need exercise.
Running with the bones of Robin Hood,
flatting my hand
where ghost trees rattle green memory
around the brute kerbs, the come-lately sodium.

They're all out kicking the ball. Wouldn't hurt.
Voices like drainage,
weasel-feet on municipal remnants.
Friends for as long as a belch
then shin-kicks,
knees on my heart appallingly,
ragged-arsers whose knuckles and shags
will get them no further
than where the bomb
callipered the Forgemaster's Arms.

Don't know you're born, you.
Oh, I do, I do,

but I hide the knowing as wafers
in the bureau leaf's running-posts,
down the back of the chair no-one sits on
where your Zal arm never thinks to swing.

You can put that face away.
This is home. Your father's settled.
Except when, as it might be at dusk,
he drives out to those new-build detacheds,
holds up a fist of money enough
to tease them off their footings—
when he looses spinach-lung breath
hard at their cladding,
magics his notes into another pint,
drinks to the health of the wallowing hippo.

Rain's back. Lucky for you, eh?
Close the door when you go,
slim the gap to nothing
against your floral outrageousness.
Tell the birds they'll taste no sweeter
than the crumbs on the mud-hollow lawn.

Who are you?
Where is your midnight suitcase?
Mine?

Zal: a household disinfectant that's been on sale forever.

In Lilac Time

(1962)

Go down to Kew in lilac time, in lilac time, in lilac time
Go down to Kew in lilac time (it isn't far from London)

Alfred Noyes, 'The Barrel-Organ'

All I remember are small rooms
the shin-level gas of dissension

the kitchen chirped once, at Christmas
a red breast beat life through the transom-pane

come Boxing Day the snow was ash
the pantry-mouse flattened its back against another year

on telly people called Askey and Ray
staggered after comedy's clean heels

at school we sang Rule Britannia
glowed from it all over playtime like Windscale mistakes

the skin of Assembly visitors
sang Castile melodies

clicked into line
like the sides of a transport coffin,

voices bittered on early fog, snot a-tumble,
we went down to Kew in lilac time
in lilac time

mom's law came sideways: a maid-of-all-work
flaring a grate inside my face

dad's was the small kid's gambit
a bonny bunch deep in my spine.

At last I shut the gate
housefronts folded behind my steps

at the crescent's end I died, lived,
broke off a billow of lilac.

Tinpot Chimera

(1963)

Day dips. My kingdom sputters.
The old fading powder fills its boundaries
and I am lifted upstairs,
lost to my unthinking paths,
the doors I swung in tiny, fierce possession.

Sometimes I creep to the landing
and peer down,
a captain whose ship was scuttled,
re-hulled, masted for an off-planet flag
while he dozed in treacherous silence.

The foot of the stairs is in fog,
patrolled by a tinpot monster.
I hear its effortful clank.
Fire from its armpits and nape
furls round the bannister-post
like the laurels of catastrophe.

Its body is patched with words
that rattle as a dowager's bell,
perform a he and she.

She chidders about banknotes,
how they play the fool, won't come into her hand,
won't pack down and build
the other half of the radiogram,
piece out a map of Guernsey
for us to say cheese in come August.

His rattles answer as smells:
bitter-and-dash, hydraulic lime,
the wide sweats of closing-time remonstrance:
Don't be even dafter, they say,
leave me get to the fridge.

I walk backwards to my room,
foot behind foot like an unengaged geisha.
The eiderdown breathes in
my regulated prayer: for empty tomorrows,
house unmonstered, my echoes splashed
about pathways and walls
till long, long after the tv says Profumo.

Caroline Caswell

(1964)

Caroline Caswell
was a gap of dawn between two fences

when her family gathered heads,
bubbled goodbye at their door

hers bobbed highest, a beauty-mask on a stick
a smile that belonged above the coping stones

the cat-curls of Michaelmas fog.
She steadied the streets

taught kerbsides their ps and qs
gentled the crack of stones

against a sleeping window
from some prodigal, keyless in the Saturday dark

delinquency pulled its cap flat to its breast
noses, for once, grew a hanky.

Her play walked heel to toe
between etiquette and storm

as a princess might sweep
clear out of some chandeliered whatnot

clip an unpriceable vase with her sleeve
leave it to rock between smithereens
and foursquare rest

I never knew another kindness
that meant itself so durably, so long.

Scratches appeared on the Caswell door
midnight tiptoe stressed their upturned bin

a stickman devil got in, hairless, yellow
took everything but her smile –

which offchance gives me now and then to picture
dropping into my eye from where chimney cowls
give up against the blue

or where tall trees
buff under that bit of spring
that's so hard to get at

Pebble Play

(1965)

Evening. The gathered day
hangs in unfinished spaces:

gateless lawn, a garage door propped
with waste metal

I work to free our house-stone, a pebble
bedded under the call-it-the-dining-room sill

if you get that loose, said dad,
head down, chin breeding chin, we're done for

I take him at his knockabout wisdom,
worry out another planet of sand,

wonder how the sky will treat us
when the pebble's gone, when I kill our life

will the street-corner shitheels
walk straight through where the kitchen lived,

knives of shadow barring oven-pad mom
from the roast she sighs towards?

will I sleep high in a bucket of air,
spud-guns poxing my bum?

inside, mom and dad laugh at the tv –
a skim of light wakes mirth

at the foot of their gulley. For a giggle's width,
they forget what they've become

but it must be done: the pebble
is now a blue half-tuber, shucking vertical ground

heat watches me where it furls like a tramp
in the garage roof's mesmerised ripples

when the pebble bounces, I'll fly up,
small myself under the heat

till nothing shows, not a tuft,
like on those best nights, Fridays

deep in the eiderdown kingdom
when school has dropped through another week
when time skins over the downstairs rages

Father Harney

(1966)

Father Harney clung to a rope
between the divines and the sulphur

struck cloven flashes from his brogues
along the aisle, up steps to an altar
whited or bloody in season

shed his December laugh
on the mulch-and-wool Nativity:

Long John Joseph, earless kine,
a card trapped on a King's remaining finger,
myurr in incontinent biro

was a purveyor
of bespoke eternities –
Good Friday gospel
sermons of geological pulse
commencing when the river broached Eden

of the abyss between catechetic demand
and our battles to answer

in we fell, always, stick-legs thrashing
Lowry out of Breughel

he approved how our shorts and dresses rode up
how we wailed our way to the tars of Chaos.

One holy day morning
his Gethsemane of boots and spears
arose upon the organ loft

where Pete Lees and I
still wearing taper-smoke
were shooting the stops like pinball:

Incredulator's cracking, Skip!
Thrust? Gone, sir. Traction? Gone.
Aw Jeez, this booster's gotta work –
Mother of pearl! Goddammit!

'What-on-earth?' Senseless words
for a pair of space-jockeys imperilled

Continued overleaf

but he spoke no further
the hirelings of his wrath
did for our crystal helmets
left our feed-lines to swing like tripe
screamed our dumbness deep in the ear of HQ

from lying Promethean upon the sun
we tumbled, bashing heads
on the nether joists of creation –
discovered ourselves un-immortalised
outside in the Darlaston Road.

We cried, rallied, discovered too
the hirelings had missed our other fire

together we pulled the pins with our teeth
lobbed in the end of days

past Mary mild's accessorised heart
the alabaster woes of St. John Fisher

the campanile belched and sundered
a man-cry beast-cry fell with the walls

up sprang the wind
we pledged we would beat it to Golgotha
place of the skull
where we'd get Jesus right as ninepence
wrap him in our blazers
proclaim him, with finger-toots, free of the Word.

Late in the Day

(Sunday, 3rd September, 1967)

Distance is smoke.
Beyond Great Bridge and Princes End
houses lock together

a model town
seen through a tunnel of doors
folds of last light on its rooftops

the Big Hilly
is now the sleep of dog daisies
summer striking all its canvas.

Dad's dead out on his elbows
my arms are around my knees –
save when the dog
knocks over our silence
stands pot-round and quivery
between one smell-hunt and the next
and his hand or mine
buffs her snout with a sort of love.

Continued overleaf

Dad and I
in baffled cahoots on open ground
pub suspended,
records and tapes,
the settled trade of indifferences –

cousins at a funeral
with photo-prompts to hand

schoolmates colliding
who cleared throats for the next word
forty years ago.

Two old fellers
come down the Hilly
trouser-hitching
bellows to an argument
that might have got going
when that uppity bit of paper
slapped Chamberlain in the face:

And the day you turn round –
Don't start all that again –
Listen, you, listen! The day you turn round –
Shut your hole, can't be doing –
Day you turn round and you say to me...

their mufflers, caps, incontinent grudge
drop below the shoulder of the hill

with a back-swinging chuckle
Dad throws their words up and over the heavens
makes Venus flare
like a goosed baroness

the dog gets in on it
ferrying a lick from his laughter to mine.

Lights are buttoned over Great Bridge,
Princes End, Hoyt, the Lost City

what time d'you call this?
is by now trailing mom like a Bisto-waft
from door to drive to window.

Upper Ballyroe, Kilfinnane

(1968, the Uncle's farm)

We stand and watch the rain.
The sloping field
strikes loose its waters
rides them down
to pools of mahogany gumbo.

The hayricks are what's left
when mountains unbuckle their splendours
fall by fall. Their crowns cave and suck.
Chemistry happens. The rotten stem
swaddles the firm.

One of us is leant against a tree,
swelling its black scars
with crooked breath, head still stuck
in last night's fuddle.
His free hand wags at his hip,
a cigarette strung on its fingers.

Someone forecasts: brighter than scrubbed beans
come teatime. Then we'll get on.
Fecksakes, the cig flares back at him,
it's torrents now, well into the boozing hour
and down to the heel of tomorrow besides.
We'll see the summer out forking blancmange,
and where were the bloody tarps?

The tarps are asleep,
interfolded like sofa cats
in the barn we walked past hours ago,
swatting off the sun…

… which someone else swears he's glimpsed,
just, way and gone over the field:
a finger of it laid underside
the gapping wounds of cloud.

Ah, he insists, it'll turn for us now.

But the sun has business
with cliffs and trawling-roads.
It slithers off (*Fecksakes*) – another kind of cat,
squeezing up space for itself
under the sag of a dresser,
or with the last of retreat up its tail
as a window unratchets and slams.

Raymond Earl

(1969)

Raymond Earl didn't have a single doorknob
in all his head

took a Shut sign to the world
save when it fed and pillowed him

or dug about for a joke he might rattle to,
a face he might hail through his deepwater light

but give him a ball and he could vapourize
the oaths of Hannibal. Thigh to foot

he drove without a car
wore down a realm of sixpences

with brake and spin. Up close,
skidding, despairing of a tackle,

you heard him prove the nothingness of words
bump noise far to the back of his throat

show that language only worked
when poured south to the engine muscles

then he was gone, leaving you
in your man-trap of turf

with a ghost on your right foot
re-tingling the jump of the ball.

He had a trial for Wolves.
Didn't fancy. Early mornings. No chips.

Last time I saw him was in the wounded hollows
of the district park

hup-hupping a World Cup '66 ball –
Bobby Moore's name, Nobby's, Geoff's and Jack's

hanging like suns the sky was made for,
petitioning the hem of an archangel's gown

with mud and genius.

A Prince in August

(Trevor Anglin, 1970)

A boy walks into a throw of sun

fifty yards ago
he slid out of a fog-stopped room –

ashtray mom with her new sprout
of woe, manning all trajectories

tile-cat sis, brother struck down
in a castor-less chair, watching

how the walls meet—the odd word
strung from the roof of his head

but not enough to pray back the telly.

A mile on and the boy
will loaf against the slow climb of stars

just off the pub's boundary
press a shoulder of underpacked bone

to a pole with a recipe for voltage
offer the whites of his baseball boots

for the sinking world to admire
wink at girls who don't come his way

channel cop show threats at some foe
who faces him invisibly down

arms a shade clear of his body
from the Bermuda of nettles across the road

if his uncle's inside, if he happens out
to flourish a piss by the tar-blocks

the boy might get a half or its froth
or anyway a whiff of the hand

that mountaineered under the barmaid's apron
otherwise it's home

his body peeling shadows hardly fatter
than the pallet-yard rails.

Continued overleaf

But for this moment the sun has him
where it lies like the slopes of Olympus

between the shop end and a mews of lock-ups
it flushes gold his penny-round collar

arrays his jacket for Assembly Rooms
the self-delighting languor of Regency sport

invites his eyes to see
how he is ruffed and prinked for Samarkand

should go there now by boat-train
by moon-fathomed roads

but his eyes fall cold and insensible
like his dad's goodbye

remember just in time to check
the last house on the right
where that mental dog is.

Thin Place

(Llan, Shropshire, Autumn 1971)

*For George MacLeod, founder of the Iona Community after the First World War, a thin place
was one where the gap between heaven and earth hardly exists*

At Clunton Coppice I coughed once, twice
and troubled nothing

twigs were fishing the wind already
a smudge on the uplands howled anyway

down in Clunbury
a pub had thrown its pork-and-spillage arms about my dad

the day would fall off its meridian
taking down his songs and money

I'd drive. Fourth lesson
gears as far beyond my robotics as ever

from here to home, the scarps and passes:
Craven Arms, Hurst Hill, Woodsetton
laying their ice against a vulture sky.

Made up of depots and rolling-yards
when did I last walk in a place like this
outside a two-forty-volt sun?

Continued overleaf

things in their quiet
got between me and my feet

goats went dainty as assassins
a horse rested its fear

on a staple-matted post, so I was inches
from a wet eye, a hulking radiance

its mouth worked like a madman's
whose tears go down the wrong way

a black quilt threw itself
across the top of the clouds

broke into a hundred shapes
of wooded preening

pheasants wallowed into their height
with the prang of Edwardian gadgetry

in one field
the afternoon roosted on a pond

another sat its frosts in a ring
like a ruckle-top pie

belly-up, a ewe cycled her forelegs
watched a pony
headless in the last fat barrows of green.

A signpost
where high road sighed into low—

broken fingers
two directions long seeded under the land

one way, my dad
distressing moonlight and roses

the other, nothing
everything.

The air thinned about my irresolution
call it the company of heaven I heard

the crump of wings
infinite through north gulley, south brake

a song without the bruise of meaning
out and away over all the wired hills

call it the year's last cluster-flies I saw
threading the road's emptiness

Continued overleaf

while my pocket-hand gripped dad's keys

dancing as skeins of prayer
while my hand let go again

dancing as crosses
while my foot beat off sudden sleet

and pounding, braced, I walked forward
walked through

resolved to give my rearing past
the slip.

Decree Nisi

(1971)

These days I sleep. You may have watched my hand
reach for the same tin as yours on a shelf.
What can I do but apologise
for my fingers' barging grasp, my fencing arm?
We no longer speak.

And yet I am much about. My body
assembles life enough to hang in step
down streets in their mid-morning idleness,
can thread steam over lightless dawn for drinks
which throat and cock in phase will attend to
while I scull through my otherwheres.

Of course there are two faces leaning in
like ignorance at windows when you choose
to eat alone. I hugely remember:
they forwarded their world to me, they set
their little angers dancing in my eyes.
Their hands loved their hips, they wore the spent light
of vestibules, shrank and wizened inside
the gospels of themselves.

Continued overleaf

It's alright. What leans in loses footing.
Each day they lie nearer forest than plain.
Some tomorrow will come with lock and wire

and I'll walk as before
my shadow in my pocket
gaze at posters for amazements
gone or never held
find sun-stones in evening hedges
watch a single swan
split the canal into fool's crystals

I'll be again the fullness of June weather
on my own land.

III.

Other Parts Were Played …

Flyleaves

birthday
between the cards
the shelf lengthens

                lopsided cookhouse:
                generations of shoulders
                in easy gossip

cloudburst
a nun's rosary
batters her breast

                sunrise in the lungs
                of Duval Street cockerels:
                the all-nighter's toast
                        Key West, 1.2.10

missing bikini-top
cigars glow
in a line of pick-ups

                steel band
                I think of all the things
                I've tried to like

Cows in a Corofin Field

(County Clare)

And so they stand,
heads up, spines bevelled.
They face their own
intimate ways,
as though each jaw
stripped and cudded
the green of a compass-point.
Clouds bag down low
about their shanks–
swatches of restless water
to shammy off
the ticks and shit
and meadow-smears
of another week
misted in dreams.

Suddenly
they wheel around,
as at a single click
up or down
in the humour of the air;
lock into the path
of a leader
who pioneers her way

to the edge of their world,
the cut of her legs
like a horse in show,
her tail a self-maddening crop.

Perhaps she has scented
a hogsback of grass
that hunkered itself
in the long caprices of summer.
Or autumn has her already
by the nose
and draws her on

to its wilds of perpetual half-light,
where shelter
is the pitch of undefending struts
in a matchstick universe,
where Novembers capitulate
in javelins of rain
on shaken eaves.

Rathkeale

(County Limerick)

This moment happens like a red leaf
blowing out of mist

in it,
a car full of soured, mid-holiday faces
clips a Georgian corner,
folds a mirror like a ricochet
with no shot to breed it
and jolts off, ancient dusts roused again,
chasing its wings

birds that cannot settle
on the bell-waves that soften the town
make for some secret place, perhaps,
where one of the shining men
laid his cowl and bones to an oak,
slantwise

an old woman, all energy steered
to the fullness of her hands –
the cards, prescriptions –
dies where she stands
from a hole-in-the-wall's shouty brightness –

gets her corpse somehow away
to an alley's last overhang

will we point ye to the hairdresser?
the ringleted tykes shinny down their question,
turn into a shriek of heels,
leave the bald man like burning stone

a lunch-hour boy,
earpiece and pecs and belligerence,
kicks the future down the street
in a shirt of gauleiter blue

the coffee-girl, late,
wakes the afternoon with her breasts
from its little sleeps
dispersed among pearl spigots – with her sigh
in which hope is just making to turn
from the last bridge of the parish

next minute, the rain,
smoking where gutters
don't quite meet the flags –
all the sea-hauling clouds
down and thick together
like tipped-off soldiery

Tintagel

Summer's here,
dipping its whites
into hours that slept happy
in the wollen seasons,
the rocky winds of Easter

that lay in rows, flush, revolving.
I sat among them
under the secret turns of fog,
the come-and-go of ice equations
where the flowers weren't.

Now shadows
roll iron through the rooms.
Ten to three won't budge
and the children's party throttles on—
onion cheeks at trumpets,
the same glass of orange
each time I look up
falling down a different hatch of space
like a helot
distracted on flat-earth patrol.

I want to rise in steam
from the leafy shoulders
of hot public gardens,
anchor in the skies above Tintagel,

where the postmistress
and the lading-clerk,
loveless through years of cargo,
of letters orphaned by bootheels or rain,
bump into each other at last.

I shall be the promenade
that opens blue
between her corsage and his gravy stains,
the engine of an evening's walk
idling,
the something that decides her daring toes,
his better-days leather.

I shall, a moment on,
be the pinch-gap
of thumb and finger
lifting ill-chosen pie from his breath,
a lifetime's disabling catch
from hers,
so words come
so a sentence outcrooks his elbow
so another hinges her resinous fingers
within it
just so
henceforward.

Lightning-Artist at Palazzola

(Lake Albano, June 2005)

Morning light
is a half-settled bird,
curious at his shoulder.
Finds itself creating
a sketch-pad
in his steadied hand –
a page of lines
that twist and thicken
as though,
tired of doing time alone
in books that are strange to each other,
they have cut old obligation
and gathered here
for the scene that makes itself
between his gaze and pencilling fingers:
a forest below a terrace wall,
woodcutters bracing and roping,
their carts halted
like winded marchers
on a route of steeps.

He dips a hand
into an hour of that unregarded world,
pulls it back across the wall,
dances the lines into shape and likeness.
Morning arcs a wing,
filches a wrinkle
from the edge of the sun
and breaks it open.
On his page,
forest and dust and cutters' backs
are fixed in gold.

Monet, Impressions: Sunrise

(Le Havre Harbour, 1872)

A laden sun
boils wax
above docks
and crating-yards
just pulling
the flesh of day
over smoky bone.
The sun
winkles deep
into boat-worried,
crane-dressed waters,
which become
a crescent of bright grief:
orange tears mass
and skitter, burning off
the sleep of the waves,
urging them apart and on
to find their tide,
catch fast to its gather.
One tear is a swordfish
that shoots the snub hull
of a pilot-boat
in which a figure
half-paddles, half-hangs
kinked in weariness,

and another sits
like a mysterious stranger
who has paid well to be ferried
to the moon of exile,
has looked his incredulous last
on the works of tears and fire.

Early moon

Early moon begins.
Jemmies roofs, swatches of furze
where towns run out of identity.

Condoles with the air
at its freight of ugliness
bred on the sun's watch:
the shut-in's cry,
the brazen rip of planes
that spray time from their bellies,
puncture tomorrow's heart.

Afternoon has caved in
to a braiding climb of smoke.
Clouds lock and pull
along disputing inclinations,
reveal the nethermost plank
of heaven,
the hole where the moon sits
dripping stars
that wake once again
to their luck of light and distance,
burst apart like unclaimed kids
lawless in a huge straw-seasoned barn.

Early moon looks well, looks handsome,
herding tides,
tipping a shoreline through a red field

seeking blowsy curtains,
a blind that rucks its linens over pots of junk –
blanching a hand within,
gingering the day's crimp of troubles
from a mouth
so it sighs and trims
furls to a buttoned rose
makes like a moon at the full –
as perfect as that
as wonder-haunted as that.

Henderson Bray's Dream Water

(Grenada – Birmingham)

At the heart of my dreams
is a puddle.
In my young midnights
it sprayed my cheek
instead of sweat and monsters.

It was a raggedy wen
smack on the crown of Marchbank Road.
Oil fattened in it like chameleon worms.
The Colcaxo girls would preen there
on mighty Saturdays,
shoving to be the queen it would choose
with a bubbled wink.
Old Dad Mazep
shot clean through it,
so it would cry its dark heaviness
away into the dust.
But its tears crept back always,
spiting the reflector
on his capering wheel.

I would ask the puddle
how it got no swell
from the rains. How it didn't crab away
to some shy underplace
when the sun whacked roof and shoulder
like a scoop
going dance to dance among spirits
on the easy rocks of Salines
at low moon.

I threw stones in it.
I threw wishes.
Nothing sucked or promised
as the wind dug about
and scarped the waters.

Now I live where roads are tame,
where murmurs of a hole
call men from nowhere
to smoke cigarettes importantly,
to frighten mobile phones.
They fuss black stew-gouts
onto the ground, pancaking them
with their smeary, racket-voice lions.

Continued overleaf

Everyone here
has to live on buried wishes.
No-one has a place
to let fall a prayer.
At least I have the water
that told the Colcaxo girls
they'd feel the sneak of an oilman's ring
along their finger.

Only sometimes
when a lagging star
shakes tomorrow down
as the scold of birds,
the first grunt of manufacture,
I hurt
from the raking pull
of its creeks beginning to dry.

C, A minor, F, G

Midwife to the Fifties
the drive-ins and rings
doused in eternity
and fools in love and teenagers
drawn to rain and zit-balm
and streetlamps like a thicket
of slouching-points
and gum to be worked
as the cud of agony
and heartbreak sparking off and on
above a lop-rimmed sink
and the rules of the hotel
and all the Johnnies and Bobbies
cock-a-hoop or lonesome
for the stretched gasp
of a hook and three verses
and all the Suzies and Ginnies
nipple-down on the coverlet
legs high and ankles locked
chin on a lattice of nailpaint
and all the future in their gaze
a blizzard of white expectation

Stars and a roof

Stars and a roof.
This is where it ends.
Night and a million downward miles
of unruly silences.
Me deep in the next garden,
hands at my sides,
the physics of what I did last
still buzzing on the palms,
hairs on the back uncertain
whether to sleep
or trade alerts with a wind
now fretting the chimneys
of another town.

I look across the fence
at stars and a roof,
at an upstairs window
where glass furls bashfully
into concave tears
as if seen from the inside of a sorrow.
Not a bathroom,
just a gap in fastness,
a call for light
and the shapes of day-birds
to broach remaindered space.

Lit now. Bits of life
going up and down behind the tears:
a ruckled arm,
a bowed head fragmenting.

An upstairs window
and voices raised,
hefting the back door open.
Something thrown out:
plastic and chime song
strung about the laneways of the dark.
A quizzing murmur.
Songs gathered, tumbled back in.
The pain of a lock,
a bolt crying you-can't-make-me.

Stars and a roof.
This is where I end.
I wait for memory
to come jaunting its lanterns.

Continued overleaf

All it lights
is a small stuffed bear
dropped over the rail of a boat:
how its paws dove-locked
at its muzzle,
how its frame of leavings
bilged and sundered on death,
as life does, mostly,
as I will not.

The leavings weep themselves
out of the past,
sink through the ground at my feet.
I follow – heavy, in a panic of quiet –
folding outside-in
like a candle never meant to burn;
rock a moment between here –
grass damp, wind hunting –
and there, where hands uncurl
to my skin, words bell down
in a colour I do not know.

I hang on my last glimpse
as a man might trouble a hill
with the clamber of exile,
taste the bitter mist
that sweats from old dependencies –

the stars cling to the roof,
pearl-mirrors turned to the westering
of another world's moon.

I've just come down a day

Close the window.
I've just come down a day
whose cold did me up like buttons,
scumbled my face with hard light.

I've been walking lanes
that might only have found
their jaggedy spaces
a moment before I struck in.
Passed houses
leaning slack against their histories,
staffed with raw people fixing gates,
runnelling the season,
whose faces came at me
panshaped and aghast
like moons from a child's pencil –
as though they'd dearly love
to see how I was seeing them
from under my less hair than previous.

I asked directions at a village store.
A voice
blew like signposts among the stock,
advising me of names fantastical,
paths dropping wide
between any compass and its tottery hand.

Had I looked back when I left,
beneath the entry-bell,
I might have seen only
a shimmered remembrance
of boxes and parish notes,
rubble asleep
in a late-day shower.

All life has been this:
blunders in high green,
in back-endish yellow.
Trespass and re-step.
Ghosts given up
at the pinch of a bend
with a dove
top-heavying the skyline.
Then, too, moments I've burned safe
in brakes of noon-coppered rowan.
My only prayer ever
has been for a lamp
to scuttle evening across a porch,
a giving door,
a request obliged in the tall quiet
about cold,
about closing a window.

How are things in Court Road?

How are things in Court Road?
How are they pulling another Thursday together?

The thorn in Mrs. Adnam's flesh
dips his peepers round the grille
of Haxby's van. He wants death back
and funning on the roads. One day,
bruises ready, he'll fall famously
inches from a just-in-time truck
and make his mother rich.

The lady with the missing letter
stands in the lounge of Unroamin.
Behind her, goodbye husband,
useless kids
echo from the silence
layered year over year
in the study-was-diner.
Before her, the matter of whether to step out
brisk along the kerbstones
pin her mouth against the weather
fill up trade doorways
like a woman with living in hand.

The Chinese student
who rents the vicar's almost-windowed room
must try out his English,
press queries of cost and distance
upon the locality:

how much in the fruiterer's
how far in U-Go Travel.
Those questions also
on old Dobie's mind,
back to the timberyard wall,
weighing a rusty bottle,
willing beauty and safari
to plume from its neck,
or a bit of love, if poss, just once.

Here are the children
who go home at midday.
Here is the eternal story:
Georgian, interwar, millennial feet
rapping on this season's make-do repairs –
inheritors of milk-floats,
of plastic strips dividing shop from stock,
tear-off numbers for losts and founds,
for doughty persons
testimonials furled
in oily or dust-peppered sleeves.

They run to where their houses wash
against the ends of Court Road,
where life moves
like an old heart
about its last excitement.
Any further would be
swan-dives into space,
shins bloodied on the nubs
of blind stars falling.

Go

(for Peter)

I will reach villages
when shadows drop just so
from spoonback clouds,
saddening the grasses
like slow, long-coated men.

I will have my times wired about me –
remembrances of Corporation pop,
of uncharactered homes
that slid through my life
like blocks of midnight freight –
ready to throw them
into dropaway rills.

I will stand and shine.
Roofs, hutments
will shine back
and I will slip on their colours
for as long as a meal,
a bed, a song that hangs lanterns
on the brewing heat.

I will stop
on the crown of a road,
with half a county
tumbled at my back,

half gone like dune-jumpers
from where my boots look.
Back along,
a potman will chase
the smell of hard words
from a Sunday bar;
cows will lean a hand's reach
from an unsober fence,
mushing the downward hours;
a bell will say six
and find no answer,
so pay itself down the steps of air,
sink its wishes
in the ruts of the lychway.

And I will be
a tide-post
where tugs and spindle-ships
throw in their cries
on ropes of water.
I will watch the sea
chop tight and loose
at a carrier's belly,
at the skimming draught
of a net-spiller
come back home.

Continued overleaf

A raft will patter down the inshore
and I will fling and spread over it,
elbows hard upon joints of beanstring.
Wait for the drag
that numbed Adam's haunches
when first he sailed his banishment
downriver.
Spin past carrier, homeboat,
birds plumed with dark latitudes
winkling salt from a pigpot buoy –
to where night-arrow stars
call me to fill their livid spaces,
shine after shine.

One train may be hiding another

(Caution. One train may be hiding another)
– Safety notice in French stations

One train may be hiding another –
a bull-metalled arbiter,
denying it flights and caprices,
staying its feel
of the speed that dreams in its plates
like the dew of a day that never heats up.

One train may steal the song
from the unfired holes of another,
even as the melody waits
to bed note against note
down the anywheres of track,
to shake the sleep
from one-eyed country stations,
jazz hanging baskets high and low
so the air is a scritch
of rusted larks.

Hidden trains
should be busy in so many places,
looping town into town
with cords of thump and skirl.
Instead they stand
in a hindward press of shadows
that settle malignant quiet in their guts,
that make them not there,
never built.

Acknowledgements

The author would like to thank the editors of the following magazines,
in which a number of these poems have appeared:

*The Cannon's Mouth, Chimaera, The Coffee-House, Critical Survey,
English, Fire, The London Magazine, Modern Haiku (US), Never Bury Poetry,
Obsessed with Pipework, Other Poetry, Pennine Platform, Poetry Nottingham,
Poetry Salzburg Review, The Secret of Salt (US),
The Seventh Quarry, Under the Radar, Wayfarers.*

'*Lightning-Artist at Palazzola*' appeared in *Still Standen*, a collection in honour of
the late Michael Standen, editor of *Other Poetry*, on his seventieth birthday
(Other Poetry Editions, 2007)

'*Pickings and Spoilings*' was commended in the
Kent and Sussex Poetry Competition, 2009

'*Uninsured*' was short-listed for the Bridport Poetry Prize, 2010

'*Caroline Caswell*' appeared in the Flarestack Poets anthology,
Sylvia is Missing (Flarestack, 2012)

A separate version of *Batmans Hill, South Staffs* is available from
Flipped Eye Publications, 2013

About the author

Michael Wyndham Thomas is the author of four novels and six poetry collections. His work has been published in the UK, North America and Europe and has been translated into a number of languages. Journals in which his writing has appeared include The Antioch Review, Critical Survey, English, Irish Studies Review, Irish University Review, The London Magazine, Muscadine Lines, The National Gazette (Tirana), Stand Magazine and Under the Radar. He is a regular reviewer and essayist for The London Magazine and the TLS. Prizes and commendations include the Bridport Prize, the A.E. Housman Prize, the Poetry London Prize and the Wasafiri Prize for Fiction.

Novels:

A Tribune's Tale

The Song of the Sun

The Mercury Annual

Pilgrims at the White Horizon

Poetry Collections:

God's Machynlleth and Other Poems

Port Winston Mulberry

The Girl from Midfoxfields

Batman's Hill, 1961-1972

Seventeen Poems and A Bit of A Song (cd)

Angels in the Telegraph Room (cd)

Plays:

FAQ

Boxed

When?

Michael Wyndham Thomas is a member of the Society of Authors and is Poet-in-Residence at the Robert Frost Festival, Key West, Florida.

www.michaelwthomas.co.uk

9 780099 277554